To everyone who has supported me along my journey

you are
important and
special and
loved even
when your
mind tells you
you're not.

When everything in your life
seems bleak and dark
Just look up to the sky
and you'll see the stars
For when everything feels
Like it's falling apart
The stars are a reminder
That even beautiful things can be found in the dark.

One more hour
One more breath
One more second
One more step.
Just take one more
You don't have to do everything today
Focus on the next step only
And just promise me you'll stay.
Stay another day
Just one more
Then another one after that
Because there's so much more to explore.
I know you want to leave
And no longer have the fight
But what's another 24 hours
The next might bring the light.
When you rest your head at night
You wish the world would take you away
Take all your troubles and traumas
But you've made it through today.
This proves that you can do it
You can make it through
I know it's so very tough
But it's something you've proven you can do.

You'll get through this.
Just like all the other times you thought you wouldn't but you're still here,
Your head may be telling you that you won't, but it just wants you to stay living in fear.
It's making you scared of the life you could have without this misery,
Because you've been tricked into believing it gives you comfort, and you just want to be able to breathe.
All you want is to see the truth and for the fog to clear from your view,
You see, this hurt you feel inside won't last forever and this moment of despair is not the end for you.
Being stuck in this cycle is exhausting and causing you great pain,
But I promise you it will be worth the fight when you see the rainbow after all this rain.
Tonight, is a hard one, I know,
But look at everything you've pushed away to get here, there have been nights you thought were your last, but it was never your time to go.
And tonight, isn't the end either despite you believing so strongly that it is,
You just want to let go of all the burdens because you've got nothing left to give.
There's not much of you left and all you want is for someone to see.
Because while they go along with their lives you feel like you're trapped and drowning in a poisoned sea.
The world you live in now feels dark and completely covered in clouds.
your mind has taken over and you've never known anything so loud.
But there's a voice deep inside, and that voice, is you.
It's louder than a megaphone and can overpower your mind too.
I know you think leaving this earth is the only way out,
I can promise you it's not. it never has been and never will be and I say that without a doubt.
You've fought through hell and back to get where you are today.
So don't let tonight and the worries plaguing your brain make you believe this is the way.
Everything seems hopeless and fighting is the last thing you want to do.
But please hold on because they're such a bright, colourful life ahead of you.
You may not believe it just yet and your mind won't either.
Because only mission is to remove any positivity and hope from your body, tear after tear.
Your journey is not over yet, there are so many paths you have yet to choose.
Don't let your mind take any more of you, this is a battle you will not lose.
Believe me when I say the future isn't something you want to miss,
So please hold on with anything you have and listen carefully when I say...
You'll get through this.

The Ache

I have this ache,
And this ache is inside,
It is niggling away,
And annoying me all the time.
It stops me doing the things I love,
And going out with friends,
Whilst they're out having fun,
I'm stuck inside on weekends.
It's all because of this ache,
The ache that keeps me up at night,
It doesn't allow me the luxury of sleep,
And many times, will wake me up with a fright.
I can't describe this ache,
As anything other than a black hole,
Too deep and dangerous to explore,
It's like a second, much darker soul.
It feels like another version of me,
Controlled by the darkness,
Clawing away at all the good parts,
Killing them with its sharpness.
This version of me with the ache,
I do not recognise,
It wants nothing but the worst,
Which it's taunts and jeers just clarify.
The ache has zapped the enjoyment,
Out of everything I do,
Why does it do this?
Oh, how I wish I knew.
It is crushing me from within,
Chipping away at all that's left,
You can stop playing your games now,
I'm not and never have been impressed.
It has made my world go dark,
And nothing fills me with joy,
Because the ache has taken over,
Its only mission is to destroy,
To break down every bit of my life,
So my world revolves around it,
So I care about nothing else,
Until the happy version of myself no longer exists.
I lie awake at night,
With the ache to keep me company,

But it emits nothing but loathing and disapproval,
So much, I feel uneasy.
It lists the things I need to change,
And alter about myself,
Makes me believe I am not worthy,
Unless I listen and do not rebel.
I feel like a puppet to the ache,
And it's controlling my every move,
More and more strings are added every day,
And makes me believe this is a battle I am bound to lose.
The ache is sneaky,
And is attached to everything I see,
What it will do next,
Is something I can't foresee.
Each day I wake up,
With the ache plaguing my brain,
I sit there and think,
I have t do this, again.
The hurt it causes,
Is indescribable,
Battling against it,
I no longer feel able.
For this ache has now,
Made me feel empty,
I'm a shell of who I once was,
And there's nothing good left to see.
I'm trying to fight it off,
But it keeps nagging and nagging,
Lingering around like a bad smell,
With no plan on leaving.
Bullying me every day,
And making me hate the life I have,
Is not something to be proud of,
So, wherever you came from, please go back.
What comes next,
I do not know,
But I know my days with the ache,
Will be painful and slow.
Though I'll trudge through them,
Carrying the ache on my back,
And hope that eventually,
The ache will leave, at long last.

You were born to be alive

You were born to be alive
Not just shrink and punish yourself
You deserve to be seen and appreciated
And not just placed on a shelf.
You were born to have fun
And laugh with friends and family
But when you're living with an illness
You can't even pretend to be happy
You were born to thrive
And see the colour in the world
The earth holds so much magic
If only you would let it unfurl.
You were born to see the sights
And what the world has to give
Not stay trapped in a life so small
You no longer want to live.
You were born to eat good food
And enjoy what your body can do
Not hate it for what it can't or isn't
What the illness says about it isn't true.
You were born to make connections
And meet amazing people
There are friendships out there waiting
This illness is not your friend, it's just pure evil.
You see you were put on this earth for a reason
And the reason is to be alive
But when you're constantly restricting yourself
You can only just survive.
You deserve to live life fully
And punishment will get you nowhere
I know the future ahead is scary

But I want to see you get there.
Because until you do
You don't know what will happen
It could be good, it could be bad
Or even better than you imagined.
But until you make the changes
You'll stay stuck where you are
Where life is bleak and cold
And there's darkness in your heart.
You're not alive forever
All life will come to an end
It's ok to fear the change
But you don't need to pretend.
That you like this way of living
And are happy as you are
Because although I know it's comfortable
You are terrified of the dark.
So why not try taking a step
In the opposite direction
So that one day you can look back
And ask yourself this question.
Was I really truly alive?
Or were you just surviving?
I can never be certain about the future
But I know it can bring much better things.
You were born to be alive
So please take a step away
It's time to start a new life
And that life can start here, today.
It won't be easy
But it will most definitely be worth the fight.
You'll get there one day soon
And be grateful you're alive.

A message for after a relapse

Falling down is OK,
And so is taking a few steps back,
It doesn't mean you've failed,
Or that you've fallen off track.
You haven't messed up,
Or erased all of your progress,
Your journey hasn't been discounted,
And you are not worth any less.
Relapse is all part,
Of your journey and healing,
I see you and hear you,
Just hold on and keep trying.
You have to fight many battles,
Over and over to win them,
I know you had got so far,
But please give it another go,
You'll get there again.
Please don't punish yourself,
For this is not your fault,
You've been fighting this for so long,
That it's just become your default.
But it doesn't have to be this way forever,
There is a way out of this,
Take some time to reflect,

And remind yourself that hope still exists.
There will be more days like today,
When you want to give in to the thoughts,
Where it hurts a little more,
And you feel struck by their force.
But this is all part of the journey,
The pain increases the more you start to heal,
Remind yourself this is something you can get through,
As long as you sit and allow yourself to feel.
Recognise the feelings,
And allow them to help you grow,
They may be painful and debilitating,
But go easy on yourself and take it slow.
These feelings will pass,
Maybe not immediately,
But they will do soon after,
Like all the times you've fought previously.
As a wise person once said to me,
You're still on track with your journey,
There's just been a bump in the road where you lost your balance,
But get back on your bike and keep moving forwards,
Getting back on your bike is what's most important.
As long as you do this every time you fall,
I know full well you'll be ok,
You will reach a time where you don't fall anymore,
But please go easy on yourself today.

YOU WERE GIVEN THIS LIFE
BECAUSE YOU ARE STRONG
ENOUGH TO LIVE IT

An apology

I'm sorry for all the pain I caused when my brain was being a bully,
For everything I've said and done, I will never be able to apologise fully.
I want you to know I didn't mean it, not even a single word,
But I know a simple apology won't take away the hurt.
See I was hurting deep inside, and my world was dark and cold,
My brain had taken over and I had completely lost control.
I didn't care about the things I should of because all I saw was black,
And trust me when I say, I would do anything to take it all back.
My family became people I feared, and I didn't believe I could be loved,
Inside I felt like a monster but all I wanted was to be understood.
I'm sorry for the way I behaved and for pushing everyone away,
I needed nothing more than you to be with me and inside I was begging you to stay.
I know I caused you pain as you saw me self-destruct,
I was only focussed on myself and see now I just needed to trust.
I needed to trust that you were truly there for me because you never left my side,
And despite me constantly saying you shouldn't, you're love for me never died.
And my love for you never went away either, although there were times when I said the opposite,
I want you to know now, that there was not a single bit of truth in this.
All the things I said came from the demon inside my mind,
It was shouting and balling all day long, saying nothing that was kind.
I tried so hard to ignore it and push it out the way,
But the more and more I did this, the more it got in the way.
You saw things you shouldn't have and I'm sorry that you did
I never meant for any of this to happen and just hope you can forgive.
Because I'm trying now to fix things after many years have passed,
I have something now to tell you, and what I say is all fact.
I love you and I mean that with everything in my body
I wish I could take back all I've done but instead I hope you can accept my apology.
Because I can't turn back time and there's no-one that has that power
But I can try my best to heal the broken parts and from now on, I'll be better.
I'm sorry for all I did, I really truly mean that.
All I can say now is I love you and please know this is a fact.

It's ok

It's ok to feel sad
And it's ok to wonder why
You don't need a reason
And sometimes there's not one to find.
It's ok to not know
And it's ok to feel uncertain
You can't figure out everything at once
No one can, not one single person.
It's ok to feel alone
And it's more than ok to cry
Isolation is a confusing feeling
And sometimes you just need time.
It's ok to make mistakes
And it's ok to make them again
They're there for us to learn from
Helping us to grow is their only intent.
Its ok to put yourself first
And its ok to let people down
Your own health is more important
Despite what others say around.
It's to have days off
And its ok to take a break
So show yourself some care
Drop your work and find an escape.
It's ok to feel lost
And it's ok to feel defeated
Sometime life doesn't go how you planned
But I promise one day you will beat this.
It's ok if you don't believe this
And its ok if you need time
No one can pressure and push you
Taking things at your own pace is not a crime.
So now you've listened and heard
That its ok to feel all these things,
I know that one day you'll find hope
And once again, see the joys life has to bring.

A message about life with an eating disorder

A life with an eating disorder
Is one that's oh so bleak
It consumes every minute of every hour
Of every day of every week
Your world is centred around nothing
But the thoughts, actions, and behaviours
Everyone becomes the enemy
And no one but you can be the saviour
But it's hard to save yourself
When you're being made to do the opposite.
You can try for years and years to work it out
And still never find what causes it.
You don't live with an eating disorder,
You merely just survive
Believing that the damage won't do anything
Because you've got infinite lives.
It tricks you into believing you're invincible
And what you're doing is causing no harm
But the harm is not just physical
And that's what should cause alarm.
For eating disorders are mental illnesses
And are so commonly hidden away
Out of fear of stereotypes and stigma,
People become too afraid to say.
That they're brain is fighting against them
And telling them to tear themselves down
That by listening to the eating disorders commands,
They'll eventually be presented with a crown.
But eating disorders just lie
And are incredibly deceiving
No words it speaks are true
Yet so many people are tricked into believing.
With every trick it plays,

The eating disorder grows stronger
Taking more life away from the person
Until they can't fight any longer.
It doesn't take long to get to this point
Because eating disorders act so quick
They pretend to be a friend
And say any problem they can fix.
But they don't fix problems,
They only make more
Numbing the original issue instead
And pushing it to the floor.
The comfort of the routines
Takes away any previous pain
Making you believe everything is fine
And it's all gone away.
But while these problems have gone,
More and more are silently building
Any sign of life gets drained from your world
And you are left just existing.
Eating disorders are not fun
And are not something to be taken lightly.
The way they can take control of a whole human life,
Is so incredibly frightening.
A life with an eating disorder
Is no life at all
It won't help you succeed
It will only make you fall.
But no matter what it makes you believe,
It is in no way a life sentence
For it is possible to come out the other side
And begin a new life of acceptance.
The eating disorder is nothing short of a liar
And nothing it says is true
And the most important thing to remember
Is the eating disorder is not you.

there is nothing more
beautiful than when
you prove to yourself
just how strong
you are

You won't always be alone

You tell yourself you're unlovable,
And that's you're destined to be alone,
But perhaps you're just scared,
Of no longer being on your own.
You tell yourself you don't need anyone,
And you're fine by yourself,
But maybe you don't want to believe,
That having someone is the best help.
Accepting that a life alone,
Is one you are going to live,
Is so much easier to do,
Then wait for someone else to give.
To give you what you need and deserve,
But something like that is never certain,
So you stay comfortable with being alone,
And close every single curtain.
You find it easier to say you're broken,
And to shut everyone out,
Than let someone into your heart,
And give them the chance to break it throughout.
Being alone is now comfortable,
And anything different fills you with fear,

Because for years it's just been you,
Since everyone before just disappeared.
You tell yourself it's because of you,
And have now put all your guards up,
You won't let anyone leave again,
So you stop it before it can get started.
Trust is something you struggle with,
As a result of events from the past,
Everyone you loved just left,
And now believe all your relationships won't last.
But I promise it's ok to let you guard down,
And open up your heart again,
Because although admitting you need someone is harder than accepting you don't,
Shutting out those who truly love you will only cause you more pain.
You tell yourself you're unlovable,
And you don't need anyone,
But In reality, you are so loveable,
And your life is not done.
Please don't push anyone else away,
Deep down you know you need them,
These people are truly here to stay,
So now please open up your heart again.

Putting yourself first

You have to put yourself first,
Although I know it's hard to do,
You care so much for others,
But it's time you cared for you.
You can't always fix everyone,
And some don't want to be fixed,
You weren't born to be a healer,
Don't be fooled by your mind's tricks.
You've spent so much time,
And given so much of yourself to others,
That there's no time left for you,
And your life has lost its colours.
But I promise you they will come back,
Once you readjust your focus,
And realise that you need care too,
It's ok if this change makes you nervous.
Changing your ways,
Is a hard thing to do,
But I promise you'll be ok,
This is something you must pursue.
I know you want to help,
But recognise that you're tired,
You have to let this go for now,
What you've already done is to be admired.
It's time to let people down,
As hard as that may be,
You're not a bad person for doing this,
Despite what others make you believe.
You are the most important person in your life,

And you can never be replaced,
So show yourself some care and love,
And don't let your life go to waste.
I know you'll continue to worry,
About what will happen to those you helped,
But I promise they'll be ok,
Now please focus on yourself.
Some people may leave,
As a result of your actions,
But that doesn't mean you're wrong,
Please don't be swayed by others' reactions.
For they really don't matter,
As long as you're ok,
This change won't be easy to do,
But just take it day by day.
There will come a time,
When you can open up your arms again,
When you've worked on yourself,
And you're in a better place.
But for now it's ok,
To take a step back,
Sit yourself down,
And take the weight off your back.
Everything will be ok,
People will understand in time,
Now let yourself breathe,
And settle your own mind.
I know it's scary,
And no is hard for you to say,
But it's what you must do,
So that soon you'll feel ok.

Recovering from an addiction

Letting go of something that's been a part of your life for a long time is one of the hardest things you'll ever have to do.
But in order to move on with your life there are some things you just have to lose.
This endless cycle is just hurting you over and over and you feel like you can't stop.
But that's the thing with a cycle, it can be interrupted and can also be forgot.
You've been trapped by this addiction for a very long time
It has you in its grasp and you're entangled in its vines.
No matter how many times you try to escape, you somehow always get pulled back.
It is manipulative and evil and the movement you give into it, you're sucked back into its trap.
You've been made to believe it's a friend and is guiding you the right way
But its words are all lies, and it has nothing helpful or kind to say.
Don't be fooled into thinking you'll be this way forever
You can and will stop even though you feel at the end of your tether.
Recovering from an addiction of any kind is painful
But please stay hopeful because it is possible.
I know it doesn't seem like it when you've been stuck for many years
When it's given you a false sense of comfort and caused you to shed endless amounts of tears.
It has control over your life and power it should not hold
Whispering nothing but abuse and lies making your heart feel cold.

It tells you you're worthless and have failed if you don't listen to its demands.
You feel enslaved to this addiction and your life has been taken out of your hands.
It tells you this is the way out of how you feel inside your head
But the shouting never goes away and causes even more tears to be shed.
There is a temporary relief from giving into the addiction
But this will never truly last and will only lead to more self-destruction.
You don't know where it came from and ask why it chose you
But sometime there is no reason although I know you wish you knew.
It is your way of coping with what's going on inside your head.
And a way of making the difficult times feel less heavy when it's time to go to bed.
But while you've been doing this the weight has only gotten heavier
But the less and less you give in to it, fighting the urges will become easier.
It's time to let go now, it's gone on long enough
The recovery will be long and slow and will be so incredibly tough.
But you have shown you have the strength to get through it by still being here after battling so long
This is the biggest hurdle you'll have to face but you can get over it because you're strong.
Addiction and self-destruction are not written in the next part of your story
I know you can't yet but soon you'll start to see.
That you can live a life without it and find other ways to cope.
There are many people around who will help you find the hope.
This is a battle you can fight and one day you will win.
So although it's going to be hard, start your fight today and please...
Don't give in.

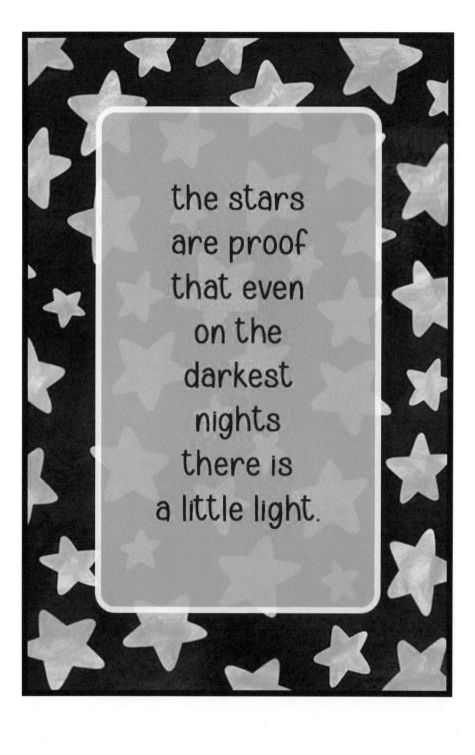

the stars
are proof
that even
on the
darkest
nights
there is
a little light.

A message about rock bottom

I have this feeling deep inside,
It's a feeling of falling apart.
I've tried to stop it happening,
But this feeling is in my heart.
I've been falling for a long time,
But have never hit the ground.
Every day I wonder when the falling will stop,
And happiness will again be found.
There used to be days where the falling stopped,
And I just hovered in the air.
Where I wasn't surrounded by darkness,
And the fight was still there.
But these days no longer occur,
And I'm falling faster every day,
Part of me is waiting to hit rock bottom,
Hoping that maybe it will be today.
So then I can start the final climb,
And get out of this hole for good,
Because when I reached rock bottom,
Fighting is something I promised I would.
But that's the problem with rock bottoms,
There's always a rockier one to be found,
I'm left clueless and confused,
And feeling like I'm walking on unsteady ground.
I realise I can't keep waiting to hit rock bottom,
In order to start my fight,
Because that day may never come,
And if I do, I may never find the light.
I will make it out of this hole,
And the falling will eventually stop,
Though I must understand, there will be trips along the way,
And many days where I fear the drop.
But I must never lose sight of the end goal,
And forget about the search for rock bottom,
Because with time I will get out of the hole,
And all the falling will be forgotten.

A message for when you're feeling behind

There's no such thing as being behind in life.
You are exactly where you are meant to be.
It's your life and no one else's
but I know it may take a while to see
Life is not one size fits all,
It comes in such a wide range of shapes, colours, and sizes.
It is something no one can plan or predict
And each life will hold so many surprises.
You may not be where you want to be
But that's more than normal and completely ok
It may take you a little while longer to get there
And in the meantime, please don't pressure yourself to into reaching that place today.
The world puts this massive pressure on you
To be at a certain point at a certain time
Please don't be bullied into believing this is what's best
Not everyone's life is built from the same pattern or design
You may be looking around at others
And comparing the lives you have
But just like we all have a different appearance and personality,
Our journeys do too, and you should never regret or be ashamed of taking a different path.
Some people may be getting married

and starting a family at the age of 20
Whilst others want to study
and wait until after graduating.
Both will find happiness,
In a form that's special and unique to them
It means something different to every one person
And if it doesn't work out the first time, there's no harm in trying again.
There's no right or wrong way
to complete this thing called life
We're all going through this together
We couldn't be telling people how their lives should look
based on what we believe is right.
The battles you have faced to get to where you are
Should have beaten you but instead, you won
So when you find yourself feeling defeated
Look at everything you've already overcome
Don't compare who are
to the people you see around you
You don't have to be anything at any age
You are your own person and what matters is that you're happy
Because when you're true to yourself and accept who you are
That's when you'll begin to see
You're not behind,
You're exactly where you're meant to be.

A message to the helper

She opens up her arms to everyone,
Gives them a safe space to talk and breathe.
She's there every second of every day,
Giving advice and helping their pain to ease.
She constantly reminds them they are worthy and loved,
And that she will always stand by their side.
Shining her torch to guide them away,
From the darkness inside their mind.
She tells them it will be ok,
That everything will work out in time.
That they may not see it right now,
But one day, the storms will pass, and the sun will start to shine.
Step by step tings will start to change,
And although it won't happen overnight,
She'll always be there to hold their hand,
And join them in the fight.
But through all her efforts to help others,
Despite all her positivity and hope.
She can't see the light herself,
And she too is struggling to cope.
They see her as the saviour,
The one who is always so strong.
But inside the darkness plagues her too,
And has done all along.
She is giving everything to fix others,
Taking their burdens away and helping them to heal.
But her hands are shaking too,
And she has wounds of her own that she needs to seal.
The pain she has pushed down for so long,
Is now rising to the surface.
It is no longer something she can dismiss,
By saying helping other people is her purpose.
She knows it's time to focus on her own healing,
And giver herself the love and care she so desperately needs.
Because while she's spent so long being the helper,
She knows she can't fix the wounds of others while her own continue to bleed.
So while putting her needs first,
May push people away.
This is what she has got to do,
So that one day she'll feel ok.

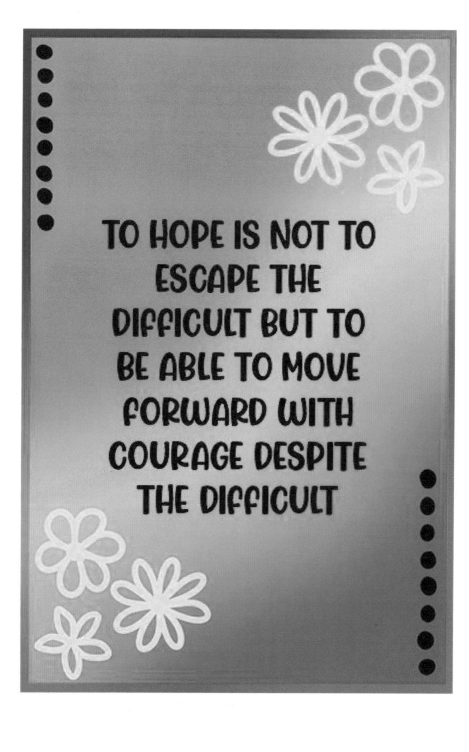

TO HOPE IS NOT TO
ESCAPE THE
DIFFICULT BUT TO
BE ABLE TO MOVE
FORWARD WITH
COURAGE DESPITE
THE DIFFICULT

To the author of my story

To the author of my story,
May I ask a few questions,
Because there are many in my head,
And I'll need you to be patient.
Lately the pages of my book,
Have been getting a little messy,
The words more violent,
And the letters less friendly.
Is there a reason for this,
Please author let me know,
Because this story is worrying me,
And right now I need you to show.
I need you to show me where this is going,
And if this darkness will turn good,
Will the next page be a brighter one,
If I could skip to the end I would.
I ask you kindly,
Why have you written such harsh words,
I don't want to hear them anymore,
There are many others I would prefer.
For they are getting inside my head,
And my mind is not treating me well,

It is confirming the words on these pages,
And life is becoming a living hell.
Did you mean for this to be the plot,
And for me to feel this way,
Was it destined from the start,
And is it here to stay.
There have been pages like this before,
But they've always been turned over,
The bad guy never lingers,
And the good one is the main character.
At least I'd like to think they are,
And I thought they should be me,
But lately I've not been feeling too good,
You are drowning me in misery.
But Maybe I should be asking,
If it's you that feels ok,
Do you need some time to talk,
Is there a reason you're writing this way.
I have time to be with you,
And will stay while you explain,
I'll be around the whole night,
And hold the umbrella in the rain.
For I know despite your words,
Written on these pages of my story,
You have my best interests at heart,
And what you write is always meant to be.

A message about belonging

One thing I need to learn
Is what I need to achieve in order to belong
But in fact I don't need to achieve anything
Because I have belonged all along.
I've have had a belief for a long time
That I will only be loved if I weigh a certain amount
But there are so many reasons to prove this is not true
So many I could not count.
I have a belief that people only care
When I'm deep in my mental illness
When all I can see is dark
And my world is all a mess.
But I must realise that worry and care
Mean completely different things
And love is not something
Making myself more unwell will bring.
Being stuck with mental illnesses for so long
Has made me believe people being concerned is normal
I have become attached to this belief
And he lengths it drives me to go to are awful.
Being myself is all I need to do
In order for people to care
But it's hard to unlearn such a strong belief
That forever has been there.
I need to unlearn that worry and concern
Is not something to strive for
But how can I let go of something
That has been proven right so many times before.
Care and support have been taken away
One I reached a certain point
I've been pushed away and left alone

No matter how many cries I voiced.
I was made to believe that everyone would go
When I reached a better place
That may have been true back then
But in reality, that's not the case.
The people who love me
Won't leave when things get better
They'll stick around through everything
And won't leave when things get hard either.
But they don't want me to be unwell,
And they don't want to be concerned,
They want to see me happy and free,
Something I still need to learn.
Me getting better
Won't make them go away,
It just means they aren't scared of losing me anymore,
And it's better this way.
I don't need to hurt myself,
In order to be looked after,
I will be cared for, for being me,
And being myself Is all that matters.
As long as I am true
And show people all I have to offer
The right ones will come into my life
And make me see I don't need to be smaller.
For I am loved
And belong just as I am
I don't need to change anything about myself
And should give life another chance.
Love is not something
I need to achieve or earn
And I hope that someday soon
This is something I will learn.

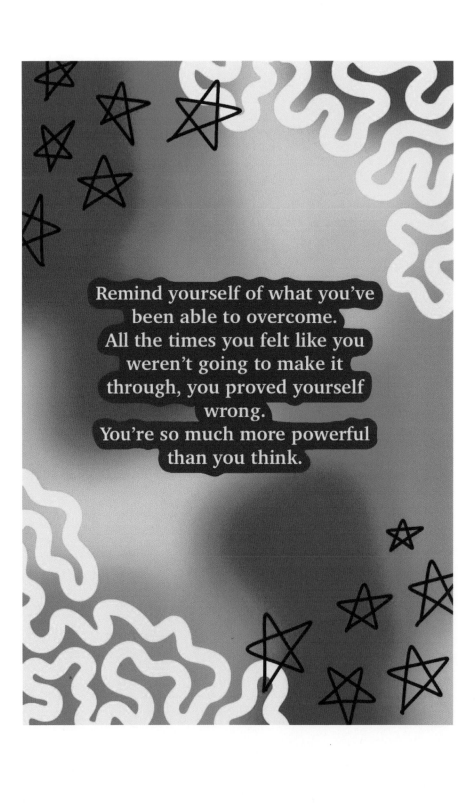

Remind yourself of what you've been able to overcome.
All the times you felt like you weren't going to make it through, you proved yourself wrong.
You're so much more powerful than you think.

A message about my monsters

I used to be scared of the monsters,
That lived under my bed,
But now the monsters have moved,
And have built a home inside my head.
I'm tired of these monsters,
They creep around and linger,
Causing damage and destruction,
Without even laying a finger.
These monsters come at night,
Keeping my mind alive and awake,
They don't let me turn of the light,
And I'm too afraid to debate.
They stay around in the day too,
Leaving my vision blurry,
Clouding every positive thing in sight,
And I just wish I could see clearly.
I wish these monsters would leave,
So I could feel joy again,
True happiness and real smiles,
I'm constantly asking, when.
When will these monsters get tired,
Of constantly running around my head,
I'm scared of these monsters,
And wish they would go back under my bed.

Reaching out for help

Reaching out for help
Is one of the bravest things you can do.
You are worthy for the care and support
What your brain is telling you is not true.
When you feel like keeping it all inside
Think back to the pain you are feeling
That pain is like a blockage in your heart
And can make you want to stop breathing.
This pain won't go completely
When shared with another person
But a problem shared is a problem halved
And I can tell you that for certain.
Keeping everything inside
will do so much more harm than good
It isn't about protecting others
I wish this was something you understood.
For your worries are hurting you
And this is what matters most
People are there to care and listen
So what I'm saying here, please take note.
I know letting people see your pain
Can be difficult and daunting
But by showing the vulnerabilities
Over time the pain will start easing.
Talking will get easier
And so will getting through the day
The first time you reach out
It may be hard to find anything to say
Because trying to explain
What's going on inside your head constantly
Is hard to do when trying to figure it out yourself

Is like exploring a new country
You don't know all the street names
You don't know where to go
It's hard to talk to people
Because what it's like, they don't know.
But you will find the right people
Who truly know what you're going through
They'll hold your hand as you explain
And constantly reassure you.
Because what you're doing is the first step
To leading a brighter life
To being free from pain and heartache
And being able to see the light.
You deserve the help just as much
As the next person you pass on the street
Everyone needs a helping hand sometimes
To get back up on their feet.
It is nothing to be ashamed of
Instead, you should be proud
That you've taken back some control
And once again making your voice loud.
So I've said it before and ill say it again
Reaching out for help is the bravest thing you can do.
You are worthy and deserving of care
This is something I promise is true.
It's scary, I know
But sitting down with a friendly face can be the start of better things
Until you take that first step
You never know what the help will bring.
It's ok if you are unsure
And don't know what to say
You'll figure it out in time
But please take just one step today.

My friend anorexia

I have this friend I'd like to tell you about,
But they're not really a friend at all,
Because how can something be a friend,
When they only want to see you fall.
This friend is called anorexia,
And it's actually my worst enemy,
Yet it gives me a sense of comfort,
And an overwhelming feeling of safety.
These feelings are all false,
And are just another one if it's tricks,
But after years and years of listening to its demands,
In my brain these feelings just stick.
It tells me I'll only be happy,
Once I reach a certain weight,
But I know that once I get there,
The feelings won't just go away.
It will want me to go further,
Until there's not much left of me,
Nothing will ever be enough,
And that's what makes it so deadly.
Anorexia isn't about being prettier or more attractive,
Because all it wants if for you to look sick,
It thrives of concern from others,
Looking ill is anorexia's biggest wish.
The lengths it makes me go to,
In order to achieve this demand,
Are exhausting and painful,
And it's scary how quickly it can get out of hand.
Comments of doing well and looking healthy,
Only make the voices stronger,
They only see the picture I paint on the outside,

And comments like this make anorexia's cries go on for longer.
Doing well for anorexia,
Means my world is centred around it and nothing else.
You lose interest in everything you used to love,
And no longer have the ability to ask for help.
Because help for anorexia,
Only means losing control,
And losing control makes the voices grow louder,
Fighting a battle like this is no easy stroll.
If you believe anorexia is a choice,
Then I ask you to please think again,
Because living a life controlled by a voice in your head,
Makes you spend your days wishing it would end.
You wouldn't choose to lose interest in hobbies,
Or miss out on time spent with friends and family,
Missing out on my teenage years,
Is not how I planned my life to be.
Days out and experiences,
Get ruined by the voices,
The internal shouting never goes away,
The only thing that goes is my choices.
With anorexia,
there are only two paths to choose,
Fight against it and win your life back,
Or listen to it and lose.
You lose everything,
Included those you love most,
It makes you no fun to be around,
And turns you into a lifeless ghost.
I never though maths would feature in my life,
Once I'd finished my GCSEs,
But turns out the teachers were right,
And I can still add and subtract with ease.
Everything I do is dictated by numbers,

They all float around my head,
I see them as I walk through the streets,
And more vividly when I go to bed.
You can't live a life with anorexia,
You can only just survive,
Spending each day trapped,
Every second dictated by your mind.
Now if you think recovering from anorexia is easy,
Then I think you need to read this again,
It is not as simple as picking up a spoon and eating,
But for someone who hasn't experienced it, it can be hard to comprehend.
Anorexia is a mental illness,
And a deadly one at that,
There is no quick fix or cure,
Recovery does not happen fast.
It takes years of hard work and dedication,
To lose habits and behaviours you've had for years,
You have to let go of the comfort blanket of anorexia,
And face every one of your fears.
Anorexia is not a friend,
And never ever will be,
The words if speaks are all lies,
Although it's almost impossible to see.
It's hard to see that something which brings you comfort,
Can also cause you great harm,
When it's been by your side through everything,
Walking with you, arm in arm.
But this false kindness always come back to bite you,
And never lasts long,
You deserve a life where you're living,
A life in which anorexia does not belong.
So don't let it make you believe,
It's the only friend you need,
Because how can something be a friend,
When every day it caused you to bleed.

For when you want to give up

I know you feel it would be better if you were gone,
And life would go on just the same.
All your troubles and traumas would leave,
And you'd no longer be riddled with pain.
But believe me when I say there aren't enough words,
To show you how much you are wrong.
I know you feel weak and tired,
But in reality, you are just so strong.
You battle with the thoughts every day,
Coming from the demon inside your head.
Giving you nothing but constant grief,
and never leaving even when you go to bed.
It tells you there is no hope,
and you have nothing left to live for
But just look out the window,
and you'll see a whole world you have left to tour.
This world seems bleak right now,
and covered in constant rainclouds.
Your eyes see nothing but darkness,
and your whole body is filled with doubt.
You doubt that you belong in this world,
and believe it would be better off without you.
Because of the way your brain has treated you,
and after everything you've been through
What you've experienced and had to find the courage,
to get to the other side of
Is not your fault,
and does not make you less deserving of love.
The battles you've had to face,
and the illnesses that plague your days.
Do not make you unlovable and a burden,
like your brain constantly says.
You've been taught in the past that you'll never be loved,
because of your struggles and the way you've managed.

That the years of self-destruction,
will cause others more damage.
What you used to cope,
in moments of utter despair
Is nothing to be ashamed of,
and despite this you are still deserving of care.
You were promised that life would keep you safe,
but that hasn't been the truth so far.
You have seen things you never should have,
and been in situations that have split you apart.
But you are not what you have been through,
and are not defined by your pain.
You have just been given a life harder than most,
along with a whole lot of torment from your brain.
This has caused you to lose hop,
that things will get ever better.
Believing you're destined to be this way,
and the hurt will be around forever.
This couldn't be further from the truth,
although I know right now it's hard to see.
When you spend your days wishing they would end,
and every second you struggle to breathe.
Staying another day is the last thing you want to do,
when getting through each one is exhausting.
Each day you fear what the hours will bring,
and facing the world feels incredibly daunting.
Right now, sticking around to see what the future holds,
is not something that fills you with excitement.
Instead, it is replaced by fear,
and the thoughts in your head are more violent.
Telling you you'll only be happy,
if you are no longer around.
That others would be happy too,
if you were six feet underground.
You believe that life would go on just fine,

and no one would feel any pain.
That you only hurt those around you,
by constantly pushing them away.
I know you feel like a burden,
and like you negatively affect everyone you see.
That no longer being here,
would finally allow them to be free.
But you need to realise that you not being here,
would leave such a big gap.
You don't see the positivity you bring to people lives,
and how if you weren't there they would just collapse.
You don't see the warmth you bring people,
the moment you walk in the room.
And you don't see that their life would stop,
and would take years and years for it to resume.
See you bring things to this world,
things that no one else can.
And have been spreading your warm heart around,
since the moment your life began.
You have helped so many people,
by simply holding out your hand.
Yet you've also fought so many battles yourself,
and this is another I'm confident you can withstand.
Your life isn't over yet,
there are so many pages of your story left to read,
You want your life as you know it to end,
but your future is something you'll want to proceed.
I know you feel it would be better if you were gone,
and life would go on just the same.
But please stick around, just one more day,
you won't always be in pain.
This isn't the way out,
although I know you don't see it.
But I promise there is hope,
and you are most definitely worth it.

A message about eating disorder services.

Something that has become apparent today,
Is that eating disorder services really need to change,
For they only consider the physical observations,
And not what's going on inside the brain.
They see a number on a scale,
And let that take the lead,
But this isn't the way it works,
So we will all continue to plead.
For a change in the system,
Where eating disorders are treated for what they are,
A mental illness and a deadly one at that,
And prevent more lives from being torn apart.
So many people are turned away,
Getting told to come back when they are more unwell,
But surely the fact you're seeking support,
Should ring many alarm bells.
Turning people away for not being sick enough,
Only increases the eating disorder thoughts,
The mind sees this as competition,
All they wanted was support.
You see levels of severity in eating disorders,
Are but should not be based on weight,
And the deadliness of the illness,
Is not determined by how much is on your plate.
Support should be given to everyone who asks,
Early intervention saves lives,
Without it, less people will recover,
This is an illness which is more than possible to survive.
People shouldn't be turned away in 2023,
When they go and ask for help,
It's not like this is something you would choose to have,
It's just the cards you've been dealt.
The less support given,
The more the eating disorder takes advantage,
And as time goes on,
This will only do more damage.
We'll see more people dying,
And missing out on a full life,
Because of lack of care and funding,
Into a basic human right.

Life is like a work of art

When it feels like the world is ending,
And everything is falling apart,
You just have to try and see,
Life is just like a work of art.
Every piece is different,
And are made with different intentions,
Not a single one is perfect,
And each has imperfections.
Seen differently by every viewer,
The meaning is never the same,
Some hold immense joy,
And others radiate pain.
You don't get to choose,
How the work makes you feel.
While some will cause wounds,
Others have the power to heal.
For every piece you come to,
You'll have different decisions to make,
Whether to stay or move on,
And deciding which turn you're going to take.
Deciding whether to remain where you are,
And observe all of the details,
Not thinking about the next painting,
And what it may unveil.
Staying where you're comfortable,
And fearing the unknown to come,
You don't know whether it will be good or bad,
But you'll never find out unless you jump.
Moving on could bring a better picture,
One that sparks a new feeling,
This work may be something different,
And hold a much deeper meaning.
It could be unique and inspiring,
And the start of something new,
Little did you know this picture,
May have been put there just for you.
Art is individual,
And no two pieces are the same,
It sparks different feelings in everyone,
It can do so much from just a frame.
When the work of art was started,

The artist didn't know what it would become,
There would be many mistakes along the way,
That couldn't be undone.
But these mistakes are all part,
Of the final masterpiece,
They are what make it special,
And also what matters the least.
Art will always be criticised,
And there will be people who don't like it,
Instead of carrying on looking at the art,
They go straight towards the exit.
If problems arise in the process,
There's always a way they can be solved,
Or to turn them into something new,
Every mistake can always be resolved.
What I have just described here,
Applies to life just the same,
It can throw everything and more at you,
Immense joy and also pain.
Life is never perfect,
And means something different to every person,
There are days in life that are better,
And days where everything seems to worsen.
People will have opinions,
About how you live your life,
But unless you value and respect them,
You don't need to take their advice.
This life is yours and yours only,
No one else can dictate what you do,
The paintbrush is in your hand,
What you create for yourself next is completely up to you.
In life there will be bumps,
And places where mistakes are made,
They are put there for you to learn from,
There's no need to be afraid.
It's ok to be a little different,
And stand out from the rest.
You don't have to perfect.
Being true to yourself is what's best.
So the next time you feel stuck,
And like life is falling apart,
Remember to sit back and think,
Life really is just a work of art.

Live your life for you.

I think something a lot of people need to remember
Is that your life belongs to no one else but you
No one has the right to disagree with how you live it
Neither do they have the power to criticise or tell you what to do.
You are the author of your own story
And the artist behind your painting
Don't hand the pen or paintbrush to anyone else
It won't bring you happiness and isn't worth debating.
Criticism from others may make you question yourself
Forcing you to change your mind
But only you know what's right for you
Sometimes the best thing to do is to leave these people behind.
You can't live your life for others
Otherwise you'll never truly be happy
You'll be living a life made for those around you
Whilst your days keep filling up with misery.
Because putting others before yourself
Will do so much more harm than good.
Pleasing everyone you meet isn't necessary
I just wish this was something you understood.
When you were a child, you wouldn't tell someone, they couldn't have the
strawberry milkshake
because you thought the chocolate one was the best
You'd tell them what you thought about the flavours
And let them decide the rest.
So don't let someone tell you not to travel the world
Because they think going to university is the better choice
Or to have a 9-5 job
Over a career that's a bit different and will give you more of a voice.
Some people will play it safe
And that's completely ok
But it's not ok for them to force this onto you

It's your life and in how it plays out you deserve to have a say.
They may be trying to protect you
Which can come from the goodness of their heart
They may have not wanted to do the things you do
And be scared of what could happen when you're miles apart.
But these are the things for you to discover
Hurdles to jump over when you get there
If it's what you want to do
Then go for it and what others think, try not to care.
It's ok to have wild ideas
And to strive for things that aren't the norm
These paths are exiting to you
And who knows what aspects of your life they could transform.
You only get one life
So you have to live how you truly want it.
Don't spend it trying to make others like you
Or squeeze into boxes that will never fit.
Your smile with always be painted
If the decisions you make are dictated by others
You have to stand your ground
And ignore when people start to bother.
When you start to doubt yourself
and go back on what you want in life
Remember that it is yours and no one else's
And it's ok to leave people behind.
If they don't understand your decisions
And make you feel bad for following your dreams
Just think back to the child inside you
Who, despite the judgment from others, chose the biggest sugary ice cream.
You've always got to think back to your heart
And what you've always wanted inside
Forget about what others think
It's only when you do this that you'll truly feel alive.

What does it mean to be 'well'?

Being well is a funny concept that can be hard to grasp.
It means something different to everyone so it's hard to answer when asked.
What does it mean to be well and what does it look like.
But I do know it's hard to get there and takes a whole lot of fight.
I think being well is the end goal of healing.
The point you reach when happiness is your main feeling.
But of course there will be wobbly times still.
Because the bumps don't stop when you're at the top of the hill.
But when you're well you are able to put them to the back of your mind.
Your brain isn't fighting you anymore, instead it is kind.
It's hard to know what being well means when you've never experienced it properly.
But there are few ways to define it which I think fit nicely.
Being well is being present in conversations and life in general.
Not being distant and lost in thoughts so terrible.
Being well means laughing with your friends about things that aren't funny to others but are to you.
It's telling yourself you're worth it and actually believing it's true.
It's being proud of yourself for how far you've come instead of how far you have left to go.
And knowing that everything will be ok even though it may be difficult and slow.
It's making it through the day without fear.
Waking up and saying, you know what, I do want to be here.
It's going out for a meal and making memories.
Instead of the focus being on irrelevant calories.

It's enjoying a movie day on the sofa without worrying about being unproductive.
Instead seeing that rest is necessary and believing you deserve it.
It's excitement about the future and all that it can bring.
And loudly singing on the drive home knowing it doesn't matter if you can't sing.
Being well is truly enjoying life.
Being grateful you are here, breathing, and alive.
Accepting who you are and being ok with your flaws.
Letting people be proud of you and welcoming their applause.
Not pressuring yourself to be a certain person or look a certain way.
Being excited about the future and looking forward to each coming day.
And those are just a few points I think define being well.
But of course there are so many more, too many for me to tell.
It means something different for everyone but is something we can all achieve.
If only we hold onto hope and every day, try to believe.
Because it's possible for everyone to truly be well.
Although I know it's hard to see when you're the opposite and unwell.
Life is hard and healing is so much harder.
But when you have a goal in mind it can make it easier.
Instead of focusing on being completely well, take things small at first.
One small step at a time and slowly the hardships can be reversed.
So what does being well mean?
Well, to me it means being happy and content.
And knowing that no matter how hard life gets in the future,
it is never, ever the end.

Thank you for taking the time to read through this little book.
It means the world to me that you would choose to read something I have
written and put so much of myself into.
I discovered a lot about myself in the process of putting this book together and
by sharing this with the world I hope that it will help someone feel less alone in
how they are feeling and bring understanding to the struggles so many people
face.
I hope that you have found comfort in the words on these pages, and they have
given you hope and a push to keep on fighting.
Always remember you are strong; you are worthy, and you are loved.
As long as you are alive, there will always, always be hope.
Just keep on fighting.
Just keep taking one more step.
You will be ok.

you have to
fight a
battle more
than once
to win it

Printed in Great Britain
by Amazon

34370055R00032